SKY TONGUED BACK WITH LIGHT

SÉBASTIEN LUC BUTLER

SKY TONGUED BACK WITH LIGHT

Black Lawrence Press

BLACK LAWRENCE PRESS

Executive Editor: Diane Goettel
Chapbook Editor: Lisa Fay Coutley
Book Cover Design: Zoe Norvell
Book Interior Design: Serena Solin

ISBN: 9781625572028

Published 2026 by Black Lawrence Press.
Printed in the United States.

CONTENTS

To my parents & to KMB—
for your endless light

"Long dark blue"
—Jason Molina, *Songs: Ohia*

ORIGIN

There's a field, wet with cricket song. There's a moon,
jaundiced in harvest. Inside me, bruised clouds

pulling back to reveal the same unending sky. Blue
kernels on the picked over cobs. There's my head,

sour with youth, in a field's grass, under a moon,
next to a prince in a straw hat. Him telling bits of a story

all out of order. I'm not becoming, but coming
out of. A moth nibbling at sugar. He says

your body is a memory which will soon have too much
of itself to know what to do with. I say,

let me forget then. Bangles of stars hanging overhead
like cutouts. Deer picking through the shelterbelt,

eyes milky with winter. It's just about to snow.
The land just about to change, to obliterate itself.

I'm ready for the taking. If only the taking would come.

ANATOMY LESSON

In the yard today, a Cooper's hawk feasting on a squirrel.
My first thought, not to startle it, to glean some
dark red truth from its oil-rig head, raw indifference,
plunging skull excavating flesh. My second, to photograph
it, send it to my father, an admirer of nature's iron-clad laws,
who once told me to let the snake finish devouring the frog,
head staring out its throat, despite my cries. Later,
we ate fish pulled from the water in front of our cabin,
so fresh the flesh swam through our mouths.
In communion, the wafer & wine become flesh & blood
of Christ. It is not a metaphor. Neither was Jonah, inside his whale.
In therapy, I say there's someone else in my body
trying to worm their way out. The therapist says
imagine your body is a ship. There's the captain & then
there's a whole crew, each one pointing you
where they want to go. In school, our teacher points
to the model of the torso. *You are mostly water.*
Jake raises his hand, asks *where does the spirit live?*
The teacher hesitates, then answers *inside your bones.*
When the captain of our football team breaks his skull,
a helicopter lifts him skyward. We shoot deer for Thanksgiving,
drown them in cranberry sauce. We play smear the queer
in which I'm chosen over & over, my body crushed
beneath a pile of bodies, a dark cave of bone, sweat
trickling into my mouth. I sob into my father's shirt.
He holds me against his chest. *This is the way the world works.*
A briny vessel, a calcium cage rocking you to sea-salt,
coarse light, until you hear the sound your marrow
makes. *This is the way the world works. Why are you crying?*

AN ATOM DOES NOT EXIST UNTIL IT IS MEASURED

until you can hear   the fish breathing   beneath the ice
go deeper   your blood   flowing   your heart
like a medicine ball   wrapped in wet socks

at the lion's den curb   tobacco spit   dyes the snow
a black   the shade of a rag   oiling a gun
whatever exists   exists buried deep

scientists admit   they've been adding seconds   to make
time work   for years   plugging up holes   in the day
when the earth's rotation   wobbles

like a tire on ice   apparently   stitching holes in time
is tiring   holding up the sky   tiring   so
they're deciding to stop   when your grandma went

before she went   she thought she was a dancer   in vegas
they say   atoms never touch   so what i feel
when i touch   the back of your neck   underside

of your knee   is a field's displacement   when you were
a kid   you asked how   they could know
it was going to snow   & then get it wrong

shoveling snow   i think of bruegel's hunters
returning to town   without trophy   heads bent
low as their thin dogs   willing their waists   through snow

while below   children played on the ice

OUTDOORSMAN

I.

My father takes himself north, after
the scent of pine bark & bear scat,
plots a course as far away from
a human voice. An ax. A canoe. Half-
pack of American Spirits. A trailing string
of lures glinting like stars. He leaves
no trace but a murmured litany
of Voyageurs. I picture him, squat
by a shore fire, undoing the jig stuck
in his palm flesh, grooved hands
etched in flame. He hopes to shed
himself, birch bark for fire-starter.
Eyelashes streaked in spiderwebs,
he walks where the pines grow too tight
to squeeze through; his body, a house
with ever fewer doors. Disappearing
into a gauze of limestone & mist. Fish gills
gaping in air. A moonbeam's echo.

II.

My mother longs for her homeland, her family,
wishes to re-crowd the horizon. A country
where only two-fifths of the land's livable.
A cobblestone city where one footstep
becomes twelve. Where the mountains are
never not there, staring back. At dusk,
we walk the midwestern neighborhood,
houses' incandescent interiors. She can't believe
how open Americans keep their houses.
No hedges, no shutters. You can see
right into their living rooms. Some doors
are even unlocked.

III.

I live alone.
Most days don't leave the house.
I am a stone wall.
A perfect citizen.
An army of one.
A trooper.
I am an open book.
Open carry.
Open heart surgery.
I hold my mouth like a wound.

IV.

A man who is not my father but wants me to call him that
sits on the edge of my bed, tells me I don't need anyone
but him. He smokes night away in the kitchen, names
the stars after cigarettes. Is there when I open my mouth,
try to speak, ask for help. He resents doctors. Spends days
leaned in the doorframe, shooting sparrows in the backyard.
There were years I craved touch from anyone, anything,
so badly, I compulsively drooled in public. The sight of grackle heads,
dew-stained in morning grass, uprooting worms,
was too much to bear. To bear: to carry, endure, uphold.
Also, to bare: like his bare arms were glistening snakes in the sun.
Or a heart laid bare is a heart at peace. My father
came across a black bear once, just the cub. The mother,
nowhere to be seen; he backed away facing it, slowly, arms upraised.
The mother could've been behind him. He would've
walked out of his body & right into her open mouth.

SKY TONGUED BACK WITH LIGHT

When the sky is tongued back with light, you'll find me here
in the peach orchard, the most I can muster. Rows & rows

of green teeth, a slab of thuds, peaches falling to ground, hands, wind.
Sign reads DON'T BITE THE PEACHES. Teeth last
past death

but decay during life. Not here, metal in a bird's shape
bearing this place's name to people who learn to say it
like a curse,

in their throats like peach pits. No, I presume that. I presume much.
Fog by the shelterbelt looks like tear gas. Looks,

but isn't. Metaphor achy under the sky's weight,
branch with too many seeds. My great-grandfather

avoided war by working on the railroad. My grandfather, college.
The worst I suffer today: sight of a bruised peach. Next
to the orchard,

a cemetery where they bury boys I knew in boxes until the ground
cataracts over with frost. Cataracts in the eyes of an
orange cat

who comes by each day to try & catch falling leaves by their sound
until my neighbor throws shoes at it. There are times

I think of taking it, calling it my own. As a child,
I'd eat pumpkin seeds & hope they'd bloom

inside me. From answer to question, question
to answer. The moment rain can be heard but the
house you're in

isn't yet touched. One of the boys used to get nosebleeds,
would lick them off his top lip. I imagine when the
dead look at the sky

it is the same sky. I imagine. Sky of shattered glass, sky
of burst capillary, sarcophagus of light. Esophagus
opening to star-stamen.

What happens to the cat, I hear you asking. Who does it belong to?

SHROUD (w/MAYFLIES & TRASH CANS)

Our neighbor of 18 years took out his trash
& was found dead an hour later
of a burst heart by his wife. My mother,
going to the mailbox, was the last
to see him alive. I receive this
through a phone, along the bank of a river
up north, watching mayflies hatch as orange
seeps through the bass belly of the sky,
everything strum in the still sear
& delicate unleaved trees.
The Dutch spent decades practicing
the precise veneer of paint
on grape skin, to let you see the translucent
clump of fruit within. He'd talked
of retirement, of moving to Florida
to be around his grandkids. This is how
we fear my father will go; the heart,
that tangerine in the chest, that fruit
turning itself back to blossom. The heart,
terrible engine of metaphor. Stretching
to hold the whole world it reaches
to the throat, the oft-mentioned lump
its vanguard of leaving the body, which is
rejecting anything that could bring it such pain.
In the river bank: mayfly molts, flecks of mica
one could mistake for holding sky.
Later, the Dutch started adding flies
like those buzzing on the trash cans
when the cops questioned my mother
to construct a timeline, a time he was here
& a time he wasn't. They said *ma'am,*
calm yourself when all she could remember
was that he always wheeled the cans around
so the lid opened away from the garbagemen,

away & not towards, away & not towards.

TIRESIAS

A red hawk kept circling high above
the hospital my father was moved to.

He said it dove past the window in morning.
I kept circling the room, thinking of when an owl

mistook his hat for a rabbit, diving at the back of
his head. A rabbit, six feet off the ground?

Some things are deadly, but incredibly ignorant,
like the nurse administering us saying

she'd never heard of hyphenated last names before.
That my mother was half a world away.

That I had slept two hours the night before
because in the back of my head

I knew his cough meant something. Other
things have a voice, sight beyond matter.

That it happened in the garden, not on the lake.
That my boss & I talked of god that morning.

When the doctor said his heart was like lightning,
I crumbled. God, let me sleep. Take

the wheel Jesus, please feed the cats for me. Great Spirit,
my father liked you more than the rest. He said

you were in bears, pines, & birds. Are you there
in his piss & blood? He said there's nothing greater

than watching a storm advance across the lake.

I saw his chest heave like waves.

Maybe there is a shepherd. That tube
down his throat helping him breathe.

But how could he know? He felt
he was drowning.

SHROUD (BLACK WALNUT TREE)

The catch of you in the mower blade, your clutching
deathrattle. I stop & bend down to examine
your black heart opened to the world. I wish
I could say I knew what to do with you.
My great-grandfather did. Showed my father
all those years ago on the farm, how to
sling shirt into basket, gather, then lay you
along the pebbled driveway for the Buick
to back over, leaving your fractured
pale green orbs drying in Missouri sun.
But he's dead now. The farm sold off.
I barely ever saw either. Little nut,
how your bristle back brushes my fingertips
like a cat's tongue. Your lacquered lungs
like the heart-rotted tree I once stood within
& stared up its trunk into light. A speckled ring,
a name in a story recounted to a child,
how to crack & cook a nut. Family boils down
so very thin. Little nut, what trees
do we stand inside of without knowing?
Whose hearts encase us if only briefly?
Little nut, teach me how to open like you.

POEM FOR BRETT

Sigh of the sun between black pillars of ash trees
falling to new nettles piercing up damp earth as I hear
your trumpet across the campground by the firepit
where you've played for my father each beer-deep dusk this trip
soft & wild like a snake unfixing its jaw my father
holds your cigarette all but a small column of ash now
burned off but still upright while from here I stare out
at the adjacent quarry it too both empty & full
with water so blue it's anything but—antifreeze
or maybe blood inside your heart before it burst
& oxygenated its first & only time many years later
playing your trumpet to no one excavating your body's
dwelling dredging whatever you could more
than you could your desk facing an open window unzipping
into that chamber of breath as I imagine now
slipping my body into this un-blue or maybe just letting go a rock
& wrecking this water's perfect awful the seconds hover
as you raise your trumpet high my father's head tilts down
down into the hard clear pure utter shatter of you—
& out your window in the yard's thickening grass the sun
sets itself inside dew on cracked black walnuts where
orchard spiders scurry between red-wing blackbird beaks
those capulets burning holes in the lawn those curt puncturing
calls like scythes of light—this blade of light just now
falling on you as you wring the bluest note from the air the light
making columns in the grass like the bars of a cage
begging to be broken into

GOSPEL

Inside the church, a sparrow gets stuck, flagellating itself around the sepulcher
I'd walk by each day & not enter. To enter would be to enter into my own loneliness.

One does not enter one's loneliness unless one has something to confess.
The church's built from trees logged around it, this other word for God: a clearing.

I kept my loneliness like a tree keeps a grub inching beneath bark, tattooing
indifferent trails like a child's fingers inside a bible, the suburbs' loosening spirals.

Winter came as punishment. We are taught we need punishment. We are taught
we must hide our money all the way to the stars, that we couldn't reach for the heavens

if they weren't so far away. I remember snow pressing against windows, at night,
in the drifts a veiny blue the rabbits dug deep into. Now, halfway across America,

deep in a different year, you say that thing which makes me cry when I can't say why.
In the bedroom's blue light, our bodies close as to break into each other. I trace

my finger down your spine & it snares around the sound a sparrow makes smacking
into stained glass, snares like a bramble in a coat collar, thuribled in pine smoke.

All those days I didn't go in. All those hours beating against light. It
comes up
my throat, a smote thing, a feathered thing. One enters one's
loneliness like light enters

a clearing. Palely. How His voice is said to flow through you. How
bone changes your voice
in your ear, so you hear yourself talking in a sound you'd never call
your own.

NOCTURNE w/LILACS & RAIN

Before rain, we steal lilac cones from rich peoples' gardens
one at a time until they make a bouquet. We go to bed

with feet the color of crushed blackberries, small stars
of broken glass kissing our soles & dream. As we dream,

it rains. Rain trickling off lilac cones like your tongue
lying limp & fat with sleep. Your tongue snug

in your mouth, next to me, & mine in my mouth.
Does a lilac like to smell itself? Is that its version of dreaming?

An unlit cop car slinks down the street, scuttling racoons
from their feast. A racoon in rain can smell like lilac, will sleep wet

curled among its sisters like a tongue among its teeth,
like bills in a mailbox. If our roof caves in

it will be because we sent the bills back
with a recording of rain inside, as if to say,

here, listen while you sleep. Hear the rain
touching the ungodly world as if this was its sole purpose.

A tremulous tongue, inventing desire.

SHROUD (BROOD X)

That month the cicadas hatched. Their flight rupturing
along our daily paths, sun reifying their rusted bronze
like long dormant lust. How else can I say it:
things that had happened started happening again.
Over our heads, blackbirds plucked their fat flying out
of the sky & we moved beyond borders of breath,
forgot the dying as the engines of our hands spread
their oils wider & wider. Certain materials don't last
under such touch, like mesh filaments of the propane
lantern on the patio, which brought them
by the dozens—cicadas, june bugs, damselflies, an orgy
of clatter, battery against an invisible barrier, a denial
of dermis—primordial reminder: anything desiring
too much ruins. Having seen it burning so long
before us, they've a story with light we can't begin to grasp.
The cacophony, the oblivion. Maybe it's all a matter of
unsheathing the ghost of yourself & laying it in the corner,
in the front yard grass, in the bed next to you. To lie
loose & fragrant as that word—*maybe*—an inside, bulb-
ous, bursting into sky, if only for a handful of weeks.

June, 2021

LOVE STORY

in the cold subway car
  you clutch her hand
& are back on
  that paint chipped porch its mouth
filling with red
  leaves burning themselves
down in a wind so cold it singes
  your bronchi, the dying fits
of the prewar furnace
  as the last tinges of ecstasy trail
through your mouth like epsom salt
  into a warm bath, the purple glass
someone takes & shatters
  over the world each night that october
which like all octobers is the last ever—
  the radio's low green glow
in an unheated Honda, the seats
  like saran wrap, a wolf's tongue
& you are clutching her hand
  thinking of how many times
you can say the end
  because what in this world lives
& dies only once
  & because when you were young
they told you the only way
  to happiness was by
holding on to nothing
  & because yes you got the flowers
knowing they will rot
  & you are clutching her hand
as the morning's comedown light appears
  & falls through the dead
knuckled trees like knives
  like fingers of the great god

of bone & you think
        i will love you with anything i have
as you clutch her hand how
        you clutched the walleye
you set free from your father's hook,
        its fins cutting open your palm
as it slides into the frigid, treacle water
        as your car shrieks into its metal
slipstream like the tearing apart
        of an atom as it hurls you into light
& what in this world isn't a hand,
        isn't a knife?

SHROUD

I doubt many would call it beautiful: this faded Lee denim jacket,
belonging to a man named Dale who worked on my great-grandfather
Melvin's farm sometime in the 60s & 70s, given upon his passing,
to my father first, bestowed upon me decades later with ceremonial
graveness, then lent for a few months to my partner—
they resewing the undone seams, needlepointing a flower
on the inside left pocket & placing their childhood good luck
coin in the collar to soothe my neck in times of stress.
I've other things from Dale—a hefty green belt & steel hip canteen
on him when he waded onto Omaha beach, an Omaha so far
from the one an hour from the farm, only to drive still further
by jeep, conferring his colonel all the way to Berlin. These
don't delight me as much as the jacket. Although I suppose
a denim jacket to be a kind of armor, displayer & bearer
of the nicks & culverts of time. How one reaches back through time
like a hand through a sleeve, the length of the familiar petering out
until nothing, gone into thin air we say, like the amount
between a body & its clothes, a stitch into its lining & lo
I am sewn to someone I've never met, who holds my father
before his 1st birthday cake in a photo undoing itself,
taken during those brief years of plenty which startled them
like sparrows from a rosebush & so touching this jacket
I touch my father at one year old, as if time were made of nothing
but endless suture, what they perhaps mean by string theory
& I fumble getting my arm into its sleeve as I fumble to get back
to Dale, my great-grandfather, my father, the quiet bombs
of bullfrogs mating in the creek that spring, translucent
geography whose coordinates arch across my back
as a constellation curves across sky; that indention—a U seam,
a furrow turning at field's edge, a pincer movement, a hug
which never closes.

ARS POETICA

after Lisa Russ Spaar

between sky & earth   the mouth
perches its heavy want

its slick parables so far from
the fingers   actual agents of ardor

i mistype poem as   *pome*
from the french   *pome de terre*

apple of earth   the earth
in the mouth   my tongue

clutching   the word   *sky*
as a shovel turns   over dirt

as the sound of dirt   hitting
a casket   the grief

of speaking   what must be
made known   &   never
understood   how else

do we   get closer
with what fingers   fail

to grasp   time's   dissolution
childhood's petrichor   her ochre
hair   o   are you

the apple's skin   or the reflection
in the skin   let me address   you

fully as i should have   from the start
as i know you   void-throat

skull-capped-window   cerulean-plowed-
field-of-nothing   cathedral-of-pale-ants

tell me is it true

waking in you   is like walking
in an orchard   where all prior

is heard   but only from a
far   opaque distance

a radio's   underwater   garble

tell me   am i   doing this right

LIKE THE SHADOW OF A WING

I too have stared at the stars & found it hard
to believe them indifferent. Who are we
to say we are new? & isn't it like this:

not what's discovered but what's been known
& forgotten, despite ourselves. Despite saying
"I want to remember this." The cold leeching

up my leg, my father's black shape
moving away through the snow, farther
from our fire ring, across the latticework
of trees. Our necks craned in wonder at the sky.
Was it this, then, the first prayer? But already

he moves further & further away from me
& I have forgotten how to move. Where,
a moment ago he traced them, constellations
fall apart like wet paper. Like the body

of the rabbit we saw yesterday slip
          from an osprey's talons & tumble to earth
                    with a gymnast's grace. & isn't it like this?

          The soul falls   catches on itself   keeps falling.
                    How when the darkness comes it passes over you
                    like the shadow of a wing.   Soft as the inner thigh
                                                            of a rabbit.
                                                                      Almost sweet.

                                                            Already
we're retracing our footprints through the snow.
Already the light has moved on. Already
we've arrived back at the fire, already
I'm forgetting everything.

GLOAMING

the trout keep coming
out of the lake forever maybe

the lightning bugs
keep to our yard embers

rising out of grass like if you press
fingers hard into eyelids *bio-*

luminescent the deet
on my skin cigarettes

in my father's lungs always
the hat of the sky

turns inside out always
his stained shirt soaks

up shadow elbows worn
thin as cicada shell always we make

these small clouds the trees
don't sound with the bodies

of the guitars or decks
they will become inside

he keeps breathing forever—
the inlet rush the shallow exit waves

on a dark shore—the mosquitoes
never run out of blood to carry

through the dark endless

brown bats crawl like paratroopers

out the eaves spackle the air &
silently thwack after

always this ticking in us
the bones bearing all night

like the lightning bugs bear
their morse code to the sky

ACKNOWLEDGEMENTS

"Origin" was published in *Blackbird, Volume 23*.

"Anatomy Lesson" was published in *Southern Indiana Review, Volume 50 Number 1, Spring 2023*.

"An Atom Does Not Exist Until it is Measured" was published in *Cream City Review, Volume 48.1, Spring/Summer 2024*.

"Outdoorsman" was published in *Pleiades, Volume 44.1, Spring 2024*.

"Sky Tongued Back with Light" was published in *Narrative Magazine*, *Winter 2024*.

"Shroud (w/ Mayflies & Trash Cans)" was published in *the minnesota review*, *Issue 103, Fall 2024*.

"Gospel" was published in *Southeast Review, Volume 42.1*

"Shroud (Brood X) was published in *The Greensboro Review, Issue 116, Fall 2024*.

"Ars Poetica," "Nocturne w/ Lilacs & Rain," and "Like the Shadow of a Wing" were published in *Four Way Review*, *Issue 28*.

"Tiresias," "Love Story," and "Shroud" were part of a manuscript which was selected by Traci Brimhall to win the Patricia Cleary Miller Award and published in *New Letters Magazine, Volume 91 no. 1 & 2*.

"Tiresias" was part of a manuscript selected by Tommye Blount to win the 2021 Undergraduate Hopwood Award for Poetry from the University of Michigan.

SÉBASTIEN LUC BUTLER was born and raised in Michigan. Recognized with the Patricia Cleary Miller Award and the Hopwood Award for Poetry, his poems have appeared in *Narrative Magazine*, *Pleiades*, *Best Small Fictions*, *Blackbird*, *Black Warrior Review*, and *The Greensboro Review*, among others. He holds an MFA from the University of Virginia, where he was a Poe/Faulkner Fellow in Poetry. He lives in New York City.